TRADITIONS OF A JAPANESE-AMERICAN FAMILY

For Aurora and Aspen – E.I.

To God – D.E.S.

Copyright © 2022 Erika Isshiki

All rights reserved under International and Pan-American Copyright Conventions. No part of this book may be reproduced in any form or by any electronic or mechanical means, including information storage and retrieval systems, without permission in writing from the author, except by reviewer, who may quote brief passages in a review.

This is a work of fiction. Names, characters, businesses, places, events and incidents are either the products of the author's imagination or used in a fictitious manner. Any resemblance to actual persons, living or dead, or actual events is purely coincidental.

Art Assistant: Amanda Ricarte
Interior formatting by Cristina Isshiki

ISBN: 978-1-7320606-2-3

MARINA

TRADITIONS OF A JAPANESE-AMERICAN FAMILY

Hello, friends!

I'm so glad you're here! I really hope you enjoy a glimpse into the life of a Japanese-American family. I wrote this book in the hopes that Japanese-American families (and all families who are interested in Japanese culture) would have a book that represented their culture and showed a little bit of their traditions at home. Thank you so much for being part of this journey.

       Erika Isshiki

p.s. Don't forget to look for the penguin that's hiding in every picture!

こんにちは (konnichiwa)!
I'm Marina and this is my home in the United States,
where I live with my mom and my dad.

"Time for school, Marina!"

"いってきます (ittekimasu)! Tell Daddy I said bye. Love you, Mama! Thanks for packing my lunch!"

"いってらっしゃい (itterasshai)!" Mama replied.

Today my mom packed おにぎり(onigiri) for my lunch and のり (nori) for snack, my favorite!

What's your favorite thing to eat for lunch?

"ただいま (tadaima)! Daddy, I'm home!"

"おかえり (okaeri)!" said Mama.
Daddy stepped outside for a minute.
I'm in the kitchen, are you hungry?"

"Yes, Mama! Let me take off my shoes and
I'll be right there."

Every night I help set the table for dinner.
I grab the plates and the utensils and Daddy gets the glasses.
Mama says soon I'll be old enough to learn how to
cook my favorite meal: rice with curry!

"いただきます (itadakimasu)!"

"Mama, do you want to hear about the Science experiment we
did in class today? It was so cool!"

"ごちそうさまでした (gochisousamadeshita)! Thanks for dinner, Mama, it was delicious!"

"Daddy, after we finish cleaning up can we go play frisbee outside?"

"Sounds great, Marina!"

"Mama, I'm going to do origami with おばあちゃん (obaachan) and おじいちゃん (ojiichan), and later they're teaching me how to play しりとり (shiritori)!"

"That sounds fun, Marina. Do you want to come help me make some tea in a minute?"

"Sure, Mama. おばあちゃん, おじいちゃん, would you like some cake with your tea?"

On the weekends I see Grandma and PopPop.

"Hey Grandma, I helped Mama pack for our picnic today. We brought some fruit and sandwiches. Would you like some?"

"Thanks, Marina, I'd love some. I'm sure you enjoyed helping your Mama pack our picnic!"

"Marina, it's almost time to go to bed.
Do you want to pick some books so we can read together?"

"Ok, Daddy. Should we read books in
English or Japanese tonight?"

"You choose, kiddo!"

In our home we speak two languages, English and Japanese. And even though this may make us a little different it also makes my family very special to me.

What makes your family special to you?

About the author

Erika Isshiki is a second generation Japanese, born and raised in São Paulo, Brazil. She currently lives in Charlotte, NC with her husband Rob and her two daughters Aurora and Aspen. Even though they live in the US Erika and Rob make sure their daughters stay connected to their family's heritage.

I'm a second generation Japanese-Brazilian, born and raised in Sao Paulo, Brazil. My father and his family emigrated from Japan when my Dad was only 9 years old. My mother was born in Brazil, after my maternal grandparents immigrated to Brazil in search of better opportunities.

Life was very tough for my parents and especially difficult for my grandparents on both sides when they first moved to Brazil. Not speaking the local language and often being made fun of just to name a few of their difficulties. I'm very proud of my Japanese roots and happy I was raised in Brazil. I'm eternally grateful for everything that my parents did and still do for me and all their efforts to give me and my sister the best life they could.

I'm also very lucky for having had the opportunity to live almost seven years of my adult life in the country where my ancestors are from. It was while I lived there that I truly started to appreciate every aspect of the Japanese culture and am now more capable of passing some of the Japanese traditions to my daughters.

I also dedicate this book to my parents, grandparents and all nikkeijins around the world. I hope that wherever you may live you never lose touch with your roots.

E.I.

GLOSSARY

こんにちは (konnichiwa) = hello, good afternoon

いってきます (ittekimasu) = expression used when leaving which means "I'm off" or "I'm leaving."

いってらっしゃい (itterasshai) = expression used to reply to いってきます when someone is leaving.

ただいま (tadaima) = what you say when you come back home.

おかえり (okaeri) = expression used to reply to ただいま which means "welcome home."

いただきます (itadakimasu) = this is what you say before a meal and is usually accompanied by putting hands together in gratitude.

ごちそうさまでした (gochisousamadeshita) = this is what you say after a meal which means "thank you for this meal."

おばあちゃん (obaachan) and おじいちゃん (ojiichan) = grandma and grandpa, respectively.

しりとり (shiritori) = a game in which the players have to say a word starting with the last syllable of the previous word said.

Marina and her family use many expressions in Japanese at home. Even though many of them don't have an exact translation, I wanted to include a glossary just in case you're not familiar with them.

www.ingramcontent.com/pod-product-compliance
Lightning Source LLC
Chambersburg PA
CBHW061117070526
44583CB00027B/3323